Rewind To the 80's
The Ultimate Music Quiz Book

Emily Goss

Chapter List

1. **Iconic Bands of the 80s**
   A tribute to the legendary UK bands that defined the decade.

2. **Solo Artists of the 80s**
   Celebrating the stars who rose to fame on their own.

3. **One-Hit Wonders of the 80s**
   The unforgettable (and sometimes forgotten) chart-toppers of the decade.

4. **Iconic Albums of the 80s**
   A deep dive into the era's most influential and memorable records.

5. **Chart-Topping Songs of the 80s**
   Exploring the decade's biggest hits that dominated the airwaves.

6. **New Wave and Synth-Pop**
   Highlighting the groundbreaking genres that shaped 80s music.

7. **Power Ballads and Romantic Hits**
   The anthems of love, heartbreak, and epic emotion.

8. **Rock Anthems of the 80s**
   From arena rock to rebellious classics, these songs defined a generation.

9. **Movie Soundtracks of the 80s**
   Relive the magic of the decade's most iconic film and music pairings.

10. **British Artists Who Dominated the US Charts**
    Celebrating UK acts that conquered the global stage.

11. **Women Who Ruled the 80s Music Scene**
    Honouring the female artists who broke barriers and topped charts.

12. **Greatest Duets of the 80s**
    Timeless collaborations that captured hearts and defined a decade.

13. **80s Music Trivia**
    Fun facts, lesser-known details, and surprising stories from the era.

14. **Rising Stars of the 80s**
    Artists who made their mark and became legends.

15. **The Legacy of the 80s**
    Hits that continue to inspire and influence music today.

16. **Deep Cuts and Lesser-Known Tracks of the 80s**
    Hidden gems and fan favourites you might have missed.

17. **The Underground Scene and Cult Favourites**
    Exploring the alternative sounds that defined the decade's edge.

18. **80s Music Influences on Modern Artists**
    How the sounds of the 80s continue to shape today's music industry.

19. **Unforgettable 80s Concerts and Tours**
    Reliving the era's most legendary live performances.

20. **The Most Obscure 80s Bands You've Never Heard Of**
    Celebrating the overlooked artists who deserve a second listen.

Chapter 1: Iconic Bands of the 80s

Questions:

1. Which British band released the iconic album *Rio* in 1982?

2. Known for hits like "Every Breath You Take," which UK band was led by Sting during the 80s?

3. Which synth-pop duo had a massive hit with "West End Girls" in 1984?

4. What is the name of the British band whose 1983 song "Karma Chameleon" topped the charts worldwide?

5. Who sang lead vocals for Eurythmics on their 1983 hit "Sweet Dreams (Are Made of This)"?

6. What Sheffield band is known for the 1987 hit album *Hysteria*?

7. Which group, fronted by Boy George, became famous with their unique blend of pop and reggae in the 1980s?

8. The song "Gold" is a famous track from which New Romantic band?

9. Which British band released the track "Don't You Want Me" in 1981?

10. What iconic duo released *Songs from the Big Chair* in 1985, including hits like "Shout" and "Everybody Wants to Rule the World"?
11. Which group released the hit single "Take On Me" in 1985, featuring a groundbreaking animated music video?
12. What band, led by Phil Oakey, was one of the pioneers of electronic music in the early 80s?
13. Which rock band, formed in London in 1977, released the anthem "Should I Stay or Should I Go" in the 80s?
14. "True" was a smash hit for which band in 1983?
15. Name the band behind the 1983 classic "Too Shy."
16. "Temptation" was a signature hit for which UK synth-pop band?
17. What group, fronted by Simon Le Bon, gained fame with songs like "Hungry Like the Wolf"?
18. Which 80s band's debut single "Planet Earth" became a hit in 1981?
19. Who had a UK chart-topper with "Vienna" in 1981?
20. Which Birmingham-based band had a string of hits including "Wild Boys" and "Save a Prayer"?

21. Which band recorded "Relax," a song banned by the BBC in 1984?

22. "Only You" and "Don't Go" are hits by which 80s duo?

23. Name the Manchester band famous for the 1987 hit "True Faith."

24. What group's 1984 hit "Smalltown Boy" tackled issues of identity and discrimination?

25. Who sang the 1982 hit "Mad World," later famously covered by Michael Andrews and Gary Jules?

Chapter 1 Answers:

1. Duran Duran
2. The Police
3. Pet Shop Boys
4. Culture Club
5. Annie Lennox (Eurythmics)
6. Def Leppard
7. Culture Club
8. Spandau Ballet
9. The Human League
10. Tears for Fears
11. A-ha
12. The Human League
13. The Clash
14. Spandau Ballet
15. Kajagoogoo
16. Heaven 17
17. Duran Duran
18. Duran Duran
19. Ultravox
20. Duran Duran

21. Frankie Goes to Hollywood
22. Yazoo
23. New Order
24. Bronski Beat
25. Tears for Fears

Chapter 2: Solo Artists of the 80s

Questions:

1. Which former Genesis member had a massive solo hit with "Sledgehammer" in 1986?

2. Known for "Careless Whisper," which British artist became a solo superstar after leaving Wham!?

3. Who sang the 1984 hit "Ghostbusters," which became a worldwide phenomenon?

4. What artist released the album *Let's Dance* in 1983, revitalizing his career?

5. "Wake Me Up Before You Go-Go" was a hit for Wham!, but who wrote the song?

6. Which female artist achieved fame with the 1983 hit "Total Eclipse of the Heart"?

7. Which former Beatle had a solo hit with "Coming Up" in 1980?

8. Known for his eccentric outfits and soulful voice, who sang "Do You Really Want to Hurt Me?"

9. What British artist released the iconic track "Smalltown Boy" in 1984?

10. Who released the 1987 album *Faith*, which won a Grammy for Album of the Year?

11. Which British rock artist is known for his 1980 hit "Ashes to Ashes"?

12. Who released the anthem "Freedom" as part of their transition from Wham! to solo success?

13. What singer-songwriter had hits with "Another Day in Paradise" and "In the Air Tonight"?

14. "Smooth Operator" was a debut hit for which British Nigerian singer?

15. Who wrote and performed the song "We Don't Need Another Hero" for the *Mad Max Beyond Thunderdome* soundtrack?

16. Which UK artist famously sang "Together Forever" in the late 80s?

17. "Temptation" was a hit for Heaven 17, but which member went on to a solo career with the song "Penthouse and Pavement"?

18. Who released the track "Englishman in New York" in 1987?

19. Which artist is behind the 1984 anthem "Against All Odds (Take a Look at Me Now)"?

20. Who sang the 1981 hit "Vienna," before moving on to solo success?

21. "China Girl" was a collaboration between which two artists, one of whom had a solo career resurgence in the 80s?

22. Which artist, once a member of Yazoo, found success with her solo debut album *Alf*?

23. What former Eurythmics member launched a solo career with the album *Diva* in 1992?

24. Who performed "Addicted to Love" and was known for his slick music videos?

25. What British solo artist topped the charts with "Never Gonna Give You Up"?

Chapter 2 Answers:

1. Peter Gabriel
2. George Michael
3. Ray Parker Jr.
4. David Bowie
5. George Michael
6. Bonnie Tyler
7. Paul McCartney
8. Boy George (Culture Club lead, later solo artist)
9. Jimmy Somerville
10. George Michael
11. David Bowie
12. George Michael
13. Phil Collins
14. Sade
15. Tina Turner
16. Rick Astley
17. Glenn Gregory
18. Sting
19. Phil Collins

20. Midge Ure
21. David Bowie and Iggy Pop
22. Alison Moyet
23. Annie Lennox
24. Robert Palmer
25. Rick Astley

Chapter 3: One-Hit Wonders of the 80s

Questions:

1. Which British group had a hit with the 1984 song "I Want Candy"?

2. What 1986 song by The Bangles became a global hit, despite them having other releases?

3. Who sang "Come on Eileen," one of the biggest hits of 1982?

4. Which British band released the iconic "Tainted Love" in 1981?

5. Which duo had a smash hit with "Perfect" in 1985?

6. "Take On Me" by A-ha was a one-hit wonder in many countries, but what year was it released?

7. Who had a hit with "Walk Like an Egyptian" in 1986?

8. Which artist recorded "Don't You (Forget About Me)" for the *Breakfast Club* soundtrack?

9. Which one-hit wonder released the track "She Drives Me Crazy" in 1989?

10. Who sang "The Safety Dance," a catchy 1982 tune from Canada that became a worldwide hit?

11. Which band released the 1986 hit "How Bizarre"?

12. "I Just Died in Your Arms" was a top hit in 1986 for which British band?

13. Which UK duo had a hit with "Together in Electric Dreams" in 1984?

14. Which artist released the 1984 single "99 Red Balloons," later covered by other artists?

15. Who had a one-hit wonder in 1983 with "Rock the Casbah"?

16. What was the title of the 1988 hit by British band *The Only Ones*?

17. Which British band is best known for the 1987 song "You Spin Me Round (Like a Record)"?

18. What song did the group Kajagoogoo release in 1983 that topped the charts in the UK?

19. Which band had the 1985 hit "Never Can Say Goodbye," a cover of a disco classic?

20. Who recorded the 1987 hit "I'm Gonna Be (500 Miles)"?

21. Which pop duo is known for the 1982 song "Physical," a huge hit despite never having another top chart entry?

22. Which Canadian band hit it big with the 1983 song "If You Leave"?

23. Which band's 1985 song "Mad World" was later covered in 2003, bringing it a second round of popularity?

24. "Wild Wild West" was a one-hit wonder for which 80s group?

25. What 1987 hit made *The Outfield* one-hit wonders in the US?

Chapter 3 Answers:

1. Bow Wow Wow
2. The Bangles
3. Dexys Midnight Runners
4. Soft Cell
5. Fairground Attraction
6. 1985
7. The Bangles
8. Simple Minds
9. Fine Young Cannibals
10. Men Without Hats
11. OMC
12. Cutting Crew
13. Philip Oakey and Giorgio Moroder
14. Nena
15. The Clash
16. "Another Girl, Another Planet"
17. Dead or Alive
18. Kajagoogoo
19. Communards
20. The Proclaimers

21. Olivia Newton-John
22. OMD
23. Tears for Fears
24. Escape Club
25. The Outfield

Chapter 4: Iconic Albums of the 80s

Questions:

1. Which British artist released the album *Let's Dance* in 1983, featuring hits like "China Girl" and "Modern Love"?

2. *The Joshua Tree* is a famous 1987 album by which Irish band?

3. Which 1982 album by Michael Jackson became the best-selling album of all time?

4. Who released the album *Rio* in 1982, cementing their place as one of the decade's biggest bands?

5. What 1987 album by Def Leppard featured hits like "Pour Some Sugar on Me"?

6. *Songs from the Big Chair* was released by which British synth-pop duo in 1985?

7. Which 1984 album by Prince included the hit "When Doves Cry"?

8. What band released the 1981 album *Dare*, which included the song "Don't You Want Me"?

9. Which band's 1983 album *Synchronicity* included the smash hit "Every Breath You Take"?

10. Who released the 1984 album *Born in the U.S.A.*, which became an anthem for blue-collar America?

11. *True Blue* was a best-selling album for which American pop star in 1986?

12. What 1987 album by George Michael featured hits like "Faith" and "Father Figure"?

13. Which iconic album by The Clash, released in 1979, became influential throughout the 80s?

14. *Brothers in Arms*, released in 1985, was a landmark album for which British band?

15. What was the title of the Eurythmics' 1983 album featuring "Sweet Dreams (Are Made of This)"?

16. Which album by Fleetwood Mac, released in 1987, included the hit "Little Lies"?

17. Who released the 1980 album *Scary Monsters (and Super Creeps)*?

18. *Hounds of Love* was a 1985 masterpiece by which British singer-songwriter?

19. What was the name of the debut album by Frankie Goes to Hollywood, featuring "Relax"?

20. Which UK band released *A Kind of Magic* in 1986, including tracks from the movie *Highlander*?

21. *Kick*, released in 1987, was a breakthrough album for which Australian band?

22. Who released the 1989 album *Like a Prayer*, known for its controversial title track?

23. Which British band's debut album *Please* in 1986 included the hit "West End Girls"?

24. *Appetite for Destruction* was a legendary 1987 debut by which American rock band?

25. What was the name of the 1983 album by Culture Club, featuring "Karma Chameleon"?

Chapter 4 Answers:

1. David Bowie
2. U2
3. *Thriller*
4. Duran Duran
5. *Hysteria*
6. Tears for Fears
7. *Purple Rain*
8. The Human League
9. The Police
10. Bruce Springsteen
11. Madonna
12. George Michael
13. *London Calling*
14. Dire Straits
15. *Sweet Dreams (Are Made of This)*
16. *Tango in the Night*
17. David Bowie
18. Kate Bush
19. *Welcome to the Pleasure dome*
20. Queen

21. INXS

22. Madonna

23. Pet Shop Boys

24. Guns N' Roses

25. *Colour by Numbers*

Chapter 5: Chart-Topping Songs of the 80s

Questions:

1. Which song by Wham! became a Christmas classic in 1984?

2. Who sang "The Power of Love," featured in the movie *Back to the Future*?

3. Which song by Soft Cell became a global hit in 1981?

4. What song by A-ha became famous for its innovative music video?

5. "Don't You (Forget About Me)" was recorded for which 1985 teen movie?

6. Which song by The Police was named Billboard's number one single of 1983?

7. "Come On Eileen" was a huge hit for which band in 1982?

8. What Madonna song, released in 1984, became a feminist anthem?

9. Which song by George Michael topped the charts in 1987?

10. "Sweet Child o' Mine" was a major hit for which rock band?
11. What song by Whitney Houston became a wedding favourite in 1985?
12. Which 1986 hit by Bon Jovi became an 80s rock anthem?
13. Who sang "Africa," a hit that remains popular decades later?
14. "I Want to Break Free" was a memorable 1984 hit by which UK band?
15. What song by Cyndi Lauper encouraged girls to "have fun"?
16. Which 1989 song by The Bangles was inspired by Egyptian imagery?
17. Who sang "Take My Breath Away," the love theme for *Top Gun*?
18. What song by The Human League asks, "Don't you want me baby?"
19. "Like a Virgin" was a breakout hit for which artist?
20. What Michael Jackson hit featured Eddie Van Halen's guitar solo?
21. Which band released "True," a romantic ballad in 1983?

22. Who sang "With or Without You," a U2 classic from *The Joshua Tree*?

23. "West End Girls" was a debut single for which British duo?

24. Which song by Queen became synonymous with stadium anthems?

25. Who sang the 1986 hit "The Final Countdown"?

Chapter 5 Answers:

1. "Last Christmas"
2. Huey Lewis and the News
3. "Tainted Love"
4. "Take On Me"
5. *The Breakfast Club*
6. "Every Breath You Take"
7. Dexys Midnight Runners
8. "Material Girl"
9. "Faith"
10. Guns N' Roses
11. "Greatest Love of All"
12. "Livin' on a Prayer"
13. Toto
14. Queen
15. "Girls Just Want to Have Fun"
16. "Walk Like an Egyptian"
17. Berlin
18. "Don't You Want Me"
19. Madonna
20. "Beat It"

21. Spandau Ballet
22. U2
23. Pet Shop Boys
24. "We Will Rock You"
25. Europe

Chapter 6: New Wave and Synth-Pop

Questions:

1. Which New Wave band released "Once in a Lifetime" in 1980?
2. What 1981 song by The Human League catapulted them to international fame?
3. Which British synth-pop duo is best known for their hit "West End Girls"?
4. "Blue Monday," one of the best-selling 12-inch singles of all time, was released by which band?
5. Who performed "She Blinded Me with Science," a quirky 1982 synth-pop hit?
6. What iconic New Wave band released the album *Rio* in 1982?
7. Which band released the hit "Just Can't Get Enough" in 1981?
8. "Cars," a seminal synth-pop track, was released by which artist?
9. What band's 1985 hit "Shout" became a global anthem?
10. Which song by Eurythmics begins with the line "Sweet dreams are made of this"?

11. Who released the 1981 track "Temptation," a song that became a staple of the New Wave scene?

12. What 1983 track by A-ha became famous for its groundbreaking music video?

13. "Enola Gay" was a politically charged synth-pop hit by which band?

14. What band, fronted by Boy George, is associated with the song "Do You Really Want to Hurt Me"?

15. Which Sheffield band released the groundbreaking album *Dare* in 1981?

16. "Too Shy," a 1983 hit, was the debut single of which New Romantic band?

17. What 1984 song by Bronski Beat addressed social and political issues like discrimination?

18. Which song by Depeche Mode became a hit from their 1987 album *Music for the Masses*?

19. "It's My Life" was a 1984 hit for which band, later covered by No Doubt?

20. Who released "Poison Arrow," a track from the *Lexicon of Love* album?

21. What 1981 single by Japan introduced their unique, atmospheric style to the New Wave genre?

22. "Situation" and "Don't Go" were hits for which synth-pop duo?

23. Which band released the 1984 song "Dr. Mabuse," known for its theatrical and experimental style?

24. Who performed "Electric Dreams," the theme song for a 1984 sci-fi romantic comedy?

25. Which band's 1985 single "Don't You (Forget About Me)" was featured in *The Breakfast Club*?

Chapter 6 Answers:

1. Talking Heads
2. "Don't You Want Me"
3. Pet Shop Boys
4. New Order
5. Thomas Dolby
6. Duran Duran
7. Depeche Mode
8. Gary Numan
9. Tears for Fears
10. Eurythmics
11. Heaven 17
12. "Take On Me"
13. Orchestral Manoeuvres in the Dark (OMD)
14. Culture Club
15. The Human League
16. Kajagoogoo
17. "Smalltown Boy"
18. "Never Let Me Down Again"
19. Talk Talk
20. ABC

21. "Quiet Life"
22. Yazoo
23. Propaganda
24. Giorgio Moroder and Philip Oakey
25. Simple Minds

Chapter 7: Power Ballads and Romantic Hits

Questions:

1. Which song by Foreigner asks, "I want to know what love is"?

2. What British band released the emotional ballad "Every Rose Has Its Thorn"?

3. Which 1981 ballad by Journey remains a karaoke favourite?

4. Who sang "Against All Odds (Take a Look at Me Now)" in 1984?

5. What song by Bonnie Tyler became an 80s anthem for heartbreak?

6. Which UK band is famous for the ballad "Careless Whisper"?

7. "Heaven" was a romantic hit for which Canadian rock artist?

8. Which band released "Love Bites" on their *Hysteria* album?

9. Who recorded "Eternal Flame," a major hit for a girl group in 1989?

10. What is the title of Lionel Richie's iconic 1984 ballad, starting with "Hello, is it me you're looking for?"
11. Which Aerosmith power ballad was featured on their 1987 album *Permanent Vacation*?
12. Who sang "All Out of Love," a love song that topped charts in the early 80s?
13. What duo performed the romantic classic "Islands in the Stream"?
14. Which song by Chicago asks, "Hard to Say I'm Sorry"?
15. "Time After Time" is a signature ballad by which artist?
16. Which song by REO Speedwagon became a soft rock staple in 1981?
17. "The Flame" is a power ballad by which American rock band?
18. Which 1989 ballad by Skid Row became a metal anthem for lost love?
19. What song by George Michael and Aretha Franklin topped charts in 1987?
20. "Total Eclipse of the Heart" was a massive hit for which Welsh singer?
21. Who released the emotional "Every Time You Go Away" in 1985?

22. What 1984 duet featured Phil Collins and Philip Bailey?

23. Who released "Lady in Red," a romantic hit in 1986?

24. Which Scorpions song is an 80s rock ballad classic?

25. "Nothing's Gonna Stop Us Now" was a hit for which American band?

Chapter 7 Answers:

1. Foreigner
2. Poison
3. "Don't Stop Believin'"
4. Phil Collins
5. "Total Eclipse of the Heart"
6. George Michael (Wham!)
7. Bryan Adams
8. Def Leppard
9. The Bangles
10. "Hello"
11. "Angel"
12. Air Supply
13. Kenny Rogers and Dolly Parton
14. Chicago
15. Cyndi Lauper
16. "Keep on Loving You"
17. Cheap Trick
18. "I Remember You"
19. "I Knew You Were Waiting (For Me)"
20. Bonnie Tyler

21. Paul Young
22. "Easy Lover"
23. Chris de Burgh
24. "Still Loving You"
25. Starship

Chapter 8: Rock Anthems of the 80s

Questions:

1. Which Queen song became an anthem of the Live Aid concert in 1985?

2. What AC/DC hit begins with the iconic riff from *Back in Black*?

3. "Jump" was a major 1984 hit for which American rock band?

4. Which Bon Jovi song tells the story of "Tommy and Gina"?

5. What Guns N' Roses song opens with a memorable whistling intro?

6. Which Def Leppard anthem features the line "You got the peaches; I got the cream"?

7. Who sang "You Give Love a Bad Name" in 1986?

8. "We're Not Gonna Take It" became a rebellious anthem for which band?

9. Which band's 1983 track "Cum On Feel the Noize" topped UK and US charts?

10. Who recorded the classic "Here I Go Again" in 1982 and later re-released it in 1987?

11. "Eye of the Tiger" by Survivor was featured in which 1982 film?

12. Which band released the 1987 anthem "Pour Some Sugar on Me"?

13. What track by Journey encourages listeners to "Hold on to that feeling"?

14. "Bad Medicine" was a chart-topping hit for which band?

15. Which Metallica track from 1988 was inspired by a war novel?

16. What anthem by Europe is remembered for its triumphant opening keyboard riff?

17. "Wanted Dead or Alive" is a classic by which 80s rock band?

18. Which song by Twisted Sister became a rallying cry for misfit teens?

19. Who sang "Owner of a Lonely Heart" in 1983?

20. Which track by Van Halen opens with an unforgettable guitar solo?

21. "Sweet Emotion" became a signature song for which legendary band?

22. "Rock You Like a Hurricane" was recorded by which German rock band?

23. Which Billy Idol hit asks listeners to "start again"?

24. "Livin' After Midnight" is a signature song for which heavy metal band?

25. Who released "Free Fallin'" in 1989?

Chapter 8 Answers:

1. "We Are the Champions"
2. "You Shook Me All Night Long"
3. Van Halen
4. "Livin' on a Prayer"
5. "Patience"
6. "Pour Some Sugar on Me"
7. Bon Jovi
8. Twisted Sister
9. Quiet Riot
10. Whitesnake
11. *Rocky III*
12. Def Leppard
13. "Don't Stop Believin'"
14. Bon Jovi
15. "One"
16. "The Final Countdown"
17. Bon Jovi
18. "We're Not Gonna Take It"
19. Yes
20. "Eruption"

21. Aerosmith
22. Scorpions
23. "Rebel Yell"
24. Judas Priest
25. Tom Petty

Chapter 9: Movie Soundtracks of the 80s

Questions:

1. Which 1984 movie featured Kenny Loggins' hit "Footloose"?
2. Who sang "Take My Breath Away," the theme song for *Top Gun*?
3. What Huey Lewis and the News song became iconic in *Back to the Future*?
4. "Ghostbusters" by Ray Parker Jr. was written for which 1984 movie?
5. Which song by Irene Cara became the theme for the movie *Fame*?
6. What movie featured Simple Minds' "Don't You (Forget About Me)"?
7. "Danger Zone" was performed by Kenny Loggins for which blockbuster?
8. Who sang "If You Leave," featured in *Pretty in Pink*?
9. What is the name of the movie that made "Eye of the Tiger" by Survivor a hit?
10. "Against All Odds (Take a Look at Me Now)" was the theme for which 1984 movie?

11. Which 1987 movie featured Bill Medley and Jennifer Warnes singing "(I've Had) The Time of My Life"?

12. What 1983 movie used "Maniac" by Michael Sembello as part of its soundtrack?

13. Which movie brought the song "The Power of Love" to mainstream fame?

14. "Stayin' Alive" by the Bee Gees was featured in which iconic disco movie?

15. What film features Madonna's "Crazy for You"?

16. Which movie used the anthem "We Will Rock You" by Queen during a key scene?

17. "Flashdance... What a Feeling" won an Academy Award for which film?

18. Which Disney movie featured the song "Under the Sea"?

19. What animated movie featured Elton John's "Circle of Life"?

20. "Purple Rain" was a song and a movie by which artist?

21. Who performed "I Believe I Can Fly" for *Space Jam*?

22. "Let's Hear It for the Boy" was featured in which dance movie?

23. What 1980s Bond movie used Duran Duran's "A View to a Kill"?

24. "Endless Love" by Lionel Richie and Diana Ross was the theme for which romantic drama?

25. Which movie introduced Whitney Houston's "I Will Always Love You"?

Chapter 9 Answers:

1. *Footloose*
2. Berlin (*Top Gun*)
3. "The Power of Love" (*Back to the Future*)
4. *Ghostbusters*
5. *Fame*
6. *The Breakfast Club*
7. *Top Gun*
8. Orchestral Manoeuvres in the Dark (*Pretty in Pink*)
9. *Rocky III*
10. *Against All Odds*
11. *Dirty Dancing*
12. *Flashdance*
13. *Back to the Future*
14. *Saturday Night Fever*
15. *Vision Quest*
16. *Bohemian Rhapsody* (Queen biopic)
17. *Flashdance*
18. *The Little Mermaid*
19. *The Lion King*

20. Prince (*Purple Rain*)
21. R. Kelly (*Space Jam*)
22. *Footloose*
23. *A View to a Kill*
24. *Endless Love*
25. *The Bodyguard*

Chapter 10: British Artists Who Dominated the US Charts

Questions:

1. Which British rock band is known for the album *Rumours*, which dominated US charts?
2. Who sang "Faith," a track that topped charts in both the UK and US?
3. What Beatles member released "Coming Up" as a major US hit?
4. Which British duo had a huge US hit with "West End Girls"?
5. Who performed the 1983 US chart-topper "Karma Chameleon"?
6. What UK band released the chart-topping US hit "The Reflex"?
7. Which artist had US hits with "Wake Me Up Before You Go-Go" and "Careless Whisper"?
8. "Bette Davis Eyes" was written by British artist Jackie DeShannon and became a US hit for which singer?
9. Who had a global hit with "Do They Know It's Christmas?"

10. What 1987 hit by George Michael and Aretha Franklin dominated the US charts?

11. "Sweet Dreams (Are Made of This)" was a major US hit for which British duo?

12. Which British singer's *Let's Dance* album was a hit in the US?

13. What band's "Every Breath You Take" was their biggest US chart hit?

14. Who had a US chart hit with "Is There Something I Should Know?"

15. Which UK artist became famous in the US with "Don't You Want Me"?

16. "Tainted Love" was a US hit for which UK band?

17. Which British band became synonymous with MTV in the 80s?

18. "The One That You Love" was a US hit for which British band?

19. Which UK rock star topped US charts with "Dancing in the Street"?

20. Who had a US hit with "Relax," a song banned by the BBC?

21. Which Scottish band found US fame with "Don't You (Forget About Me)"?

22. "A View to a Kill" was a US hit for which British band?

23. What was Phil Collins' biggest solo US hit of the 80s?

24. Who had a US hit with "Vienna"?

25. Which band scored US success with "The Final Countdown"?

Chapter 10 Answers:

1. Fleetwood Mac
2. George Michael
3. Paul McCartney
4. Pet Shop Boys
5. Culture Club
6. Duran Duran
7. George Michael (Wham!)
8. Kim Carnes
9. Band Aid
10. "I Knew You Were Waiting (For Me)"
11. Eurythmics
12. David Bowie
13. The Police
14. Duran Duran
15. The Human League
16. Soft Cell
17. Duran Duran
18. Air Supply
19. Mick Jagger and David Bowie
20. Frankie Goes to Hollywood

21. Simple Minds
22. Duran Duran
23. "Against All Odds (Take a Look at Me Now)"
24. Ultravox
25. Europe

Chapter 11: Women Who Ruled the 80s Music Scene

Questions:

1. Which iconic female artist released *Like a Virgin* in 1984?
2. "Girls Just Want to Have Fun" was a breakout hit for which singer?
3. Who became famous for the anthem "What's Love Got to Do with It"?
4. Which artist released the album *Hounds of Love* in 1985?
5. Who sang "I Think We're Alone Now" in 1987, becoming a teenage pop star?
6. What Welsh singer performed "Total Eclipse of the Heart"?
7. "Fast Car" was a hit for which folk-inspired singer?
8. Which American artist sang "Straight Up" in 1988?
9. What British Nigerian artist sang the 1984 hit "Smooth Operator"?

10. Which UK singer rose to fame with the ballad "You're the Best Thing"?

11. Who performed the chart-topping hit "I Wanna Dance with Somebody" in 1987?

12. Which Australian pop star released "I Should Be So Lucky"?

13. Who performed "Into the Groove," featured in *Desperately Seeking Susan*?

14. What singer became known for her rebellious image with "Black Velvet"?

15. "Heaven is a Place on Earth" was a hit for which American singer?

16. Which 80s star released the feminist anthem "Express Yourself"?

17. "Mickey" became a one-hit wonder for which female artist?

18. Who sang "Touch Me (I Want Your Body)" in 1986?

19. What artist released the rock anthem "Edge of Seventeen"?

20. "Time After Time" is a signature hit for which 80s star?

21. Which American pop singer released the album *True Blue*?

22. Who became famous for the duet "(I've Had) The Time of My Life"?

23. What country star transitioned to pop with "9 to 5"?

24. Who performed the 1989 power ballad "Wind Beneath My Wings"?

25. Which Canadian artist released the hit "Could I Be Your Girl"?

Chapter 11 Answers:

1. Madonna
2. Cyndi Lauper
3. Tina Turner
4. Kate Bush
5. Tiffany
6. Bonnie Tyler
7. Tracy Chapman
8. Paula Abdul
9. Sade
10. The Style Council (Paul Weller and Dee C. Lee)
11. Whitney Houston
12. Kylie Minogue
13. Madonna
14. Alannah Myles
15. Belinda Carlisle
16. Madonna
17. Toni Basil
18. Samantha Fox
19. Stevie Nicks

20. Cyndi Lauper
21. Madonna
22. Jennifer Warnes
23. Dolly Parton
24. Bette Midler
25. Jann Arden

Chapter 12: Greatest Duets of the 80s

Questions:

1. Which 1981 duet featured Diana Ross and Lionel Richie?
2. "Easy Lover" was sung by Phil Collins and which other artist?
3. Who sang "Islands in the Stream" with Dolly Parton?
4. Which Elton John duet became a hit in 1985?
5. Who joined forces with Michael Jackson for "Say Say Say"?
6. What 1989 hit paired Paula Abdul and The Wild Pair?
7. "I Knew You Were Waiting (For Me)" was performed by Aretha Franklin and which British artist?
8. "Don't Give Up" featured Peter Gabriel and which female artist?
9. Who sang "Under Pressure" with Queen?
10. What iconic duet featured Barbra Streisand and Barry Gibb?

11. Which 1988 duet paired Whitney Houston with Jermaine Jackson?
12. Who recorded "Reunited" in 1980?
13. Which hit duet featured Natalie Cole and Nat King Cole, using digital technology?
14. Who sang "Tonight I Celebrate My Love" in 1983?
15. "Whenever I Call You Friend" featured Kenny Loggins and which female artist?
16. "You've Lost That Lovin' Feeling" was a duet between Hall & Oates and which band?
17. Who teamed up for "Baby Come to Me" in 1983?
18. "Solid" was a duet hit for which married couple?
19. "Friends and Lovers" was sung by which duo?
20. Who sang the duet "You're the One That I Want" in *Grease*?
21. Which rock legend performed "Leather and Lace" with Don Henley?
22. Who joined forces for "Up Where We Belong" in 1982?
23. "All I Have to Do Is Dream" was a duet by Cliff Richard and which artist?

24. Which song brought together Chrissie Hynde and UB40?

25. Who sang the duet "Endless Love" in the movie of the same name?

Chapter 12 Answers:

1. "Endless Love"
2. Philip Bailey
3. Kenny Rogers
4. "Don't Let the Sun Go Down on Me" (with George Michael in live versions)
5. Paul McCartney
6. "Opposites Attract"
7. George Michael
8. Kate Bush
9. David Bowie
10. "Guilty"
11. "If You Say My Eyes Are Beautiful"
12. Peaches & Herb
13. "Unforgettable"
14. Peabo Bryson and Roberta Flack
15. Stevie Nicks
16. The Righteous Brothers
17. James Ingram and Patti Austin
18. Ashford & Simpson
19. Gloria Loring and Carl Anderson

20. John Travolta and Olivia Newton-John
21. Stevie Nicks
22. Joe Cocker and Jennifer Warnes
23. Olivia Newton-John
24. "I Got You Babe"
25. Lionel Richie and Diana Ross

Chapter 13: 80s Music Trivia (Fun Facts and Lesser-Known Details)

Questions:

1. What was the first music video aired on MTV in 1981?

2. Which 80s album is the best-selling of all time?

3. Who was the first female artist to win a Grammy for Album of the Year in the 1980s?

4. Which iconic pop star's famous white glove debuted during a live performance of "Billie Jean"?

5. What year did the Band Aid single "Do They Know It's Christmas?" release?

6. Which British duo was the first act to perform on the BBC's *Top of the Pops* entirely using synthesizers?

7. "Purple Rain" was not just an album but also a movie. Who starred in it?

8. What artist became synonymous with the 80s slogan "I Want My MTV"?

9. Which 80s hit was re-released in 1991 and went on to top charts again?

10. Who was the youngest solo artist to reach #1 on the UK charts in the 80s?
11. Which artist's performance at Live Aid 1985 is considered one of the best in rock history?
12. What was the first UK chart-topping song to feature rapping?
13. What 1980 hit by Queen was their first US #1 song?
14. Who became the first female artist to sell over 1 million copies of a single in the UK?
15. What was the most-watched music video premiere on MTV in the 80s?
16. Which song by Soft Cell broke a record for the longest consecutive stay on the UK charts?
17. What 80s hit featured on *Top Gun* won an Academy Award for Best Original Song?
18. Which 80s singer became a global superstar after winning Eurovision in 1988?
19. "Sweet Child o' Mine" by Guns N' Roses became the first single from which album?
20. Which 1980s star was knighted by Queen Elizabeth II?
21. What song did Prince originally write for Stevie Nicks, who turned it down?

22. Which 80s band's members included both Bono and The Edge?

23. Which song was Queen's tribute to Elvis Presley, blending rock and opera?

24. "Faith" by George Michael was the first solo album to achieve what milestone?

25. What was the last UK #1 song of the 1980s?

Chapter 13 Answers:

1. "Video Killed the Radio Star" by The Buggles
2. *Thriller* by Michael Jackson
3. Christopher Cross (*Sailing*, 1981)
4. Michael Jackson
5. 1984
6. Orchestral Manoeuvres in the Dark
7. Prince
8. David Bowie
9. "Bohemian Rhapsody" by Queen
10. Tiffany (*I Think We're Alone Now*)
11. Queen
12. "Rapture" by Blondie
13. "Crazy Little Thing Called Love"
14. Kylie Minogue (*I Should Be So Lucky*)
15. "Thriller" by Michael Jackson
16. "Tainted Love"
17. "Take My Breath Away" by Berlin
18. Celine Dion
19. *Appetite for Destruction*
20. Elton John

21. "Purple Rain"

22. U2

23. "Crazy Little Thing Called Love"

24. First debut solo album to reach the Diamond Certification

25. "Do They Know It's Christmas?" by Band Aid

Chapter 14: Rising Stars of the 80s

Questions:

1. Which artist released their debut album in 1985, becoming an instant superstar?
2. Who broke into fame with *Purple Rain* in 1984?
3. What group, fronted by George Michael, achieved massive success with their debut album *Fantastic*?
4. Who released the album *She's So Unusual* in 1983?
5. Which artist released her debut album, in 1983?
6. Which band became famous after their role in *The Breakfast Club* soundtrack with "Don't You (Forget About Me)"?
7. Which Irish rock band found international success with *The Joshua Tree* in 1987?
8. Who released *Let's Dance* in 1983, revitalizing their career and gaining a new audience?
9. What group's debut album, *Licensed to Ill*, introduced rap-rock to the mainstream?
10. Which Australian pop princess rose to fame with her debut album *Kylie* in 1988?

11. Who burst onto the scene with the 1986 hit "Take My Breath Away"?

12. What British duo's debut album *Please* featured "West End Girls"?

13. Who released *Like a Virgin* in 1984, solidifying their place as a pop icon?

14. Which band debuted with *Hunting High and Low* in 1985, featuring "Take on Me"?

15. What group of brothers achieved fame with "Wake Me Up Before You Go-Go"?

16. Who released the album *Faith* in 1987, launching a solo career after Wham!?

17. "Manic Monday" was a breakout hit for which group?

18. Which artist debuted in 1987 with "Never Gonna Give You Up"?

19. What British band's debut album *Rio* helped define the New Romantic era?

20. Who released "Touch Me (I Want Your Body)" as their debut single?

21. What band became famous after releasing *The Hurting* in 1983?

22. Which artist skyrocketed to fame with "Let's Hear It for the Boy"?

23. What group debuted with "Relax," sparking controversy in the UK?

24. Who released *Control* in 1986, solidifying her career outside of her famous family?

25. What solo artist debuted in the 80s but found more fame in the 90s with *Jagged Little Pill*?

Chapter 14 Answers:

1. Whitney Houston
2. Prince
3. Wham!
4. Cyndi Lauper
5. Madonna
6. Simple Minds
7. U2
8. David Bowie
9. Beastie Boys
10. Kylie Minogue
11. Berlin
12. Pet Shop Boys
13. Madonna
14. A-ha
15. Wham!
16. George Michael
17. The Bangles
18. Rick Astley
19. Duran Duran

20. Samantha Fox
21. Tears for Fears
22. Deniece Williams
23. Frankie Goes to Hollywood
24. Janet Jackson
25. Alanis Morissette

Chapter 15: The Legacy of the 80s

Questions:

1. Which artist's 1982 album *Thriller* remains influential in pop culture?

2. "Don't Stop Believin'" by Journey became an anthem for which generation?

3. Which band's influence is seen in modern acts like Coldplay?

4. What 80s song resurged in popularity after its use in *Stranger Things*?

5. "Take On Me" by A-ha is often associated with what innovation in music videos?

6. Which New Wave band paved the way for electronic acts in the 2000s?

7. "Africa" by Toto went viral decades later thanks to which social media platform?

8. What 80s music video is often cited as one of the most expensive ever made?

9. Which 80s pop icon is still referred to as the "Queen of Pop"?

10. What 1985 event is considered a defining moment in global charity efforts?

11. "Sweet Child o' Mine" inspired future generations of what genre?

12. Which artist was inducted into the Rock & Roll Hall of Fame posthumously in 1997?

13. What 80s anthem is used in countless sports stadiums?

14. "Everybody Wants to Rule the World" is often sampled in modern music. Who sang it?

15. Which Prince album became a blueprint for many artists?

16. What song by Queen continues to be sung at live events worldwide?

17. "With or Without You" is often cited as one of the best songs of the 80s. Which band performed it?

18. What 80s artist heavily influenced Lady Gaga's visual and musical style?

19. "Relax" by Frankie Goes to Hollywood became a cultural milestone for what reason?

20. Who was the first 80s artist to headline a Super Bowl halftime show?

21. Which movie introduced "Eye of the Tiger," inspiring countless training montages?

22. Which song was used in the closing credits of *The Breakfast Club*?

23. "Fast Car" became a template for storytelling in modern music. Who sang it?

24. What 1980s band is credited with creating the New Romantic movement?

25. Which 80s anthem is the most streamed song from the decade on Spotify?

Chapter 15 Answers:

1. Michael Jackson
2. Millennials and Gen X
3. U2
4. "Running Up That Hill" by Kate Bush
5. Animation/live-action integration
6. Depeche Mode
7. TikTok
8. "Scream" by Michael and Janet Jackson
9. Madonna
10. Live Aid
11. Hard Rock
12. Freddie Mercury
13. "We Will Rock You"
14. Tears for Fears
15. *Purple Rain*
16. "Bohemian Rhapsody"
17. U2
18. Madonna
19. Censorship and boldness in music
20. Michael Jackson
21. *Rocky III*

22. "Don't You (Forget About Me)"
23. Tracy Chapman
24. Spandau Ballet
25. "Africa" by Toto

Chapter 16: Deep Cuts and Lesser-Known Tracks of the 80s

Questions:

1. What 1981 album by David Bowie featured the song "Wild Is the Wind"?

2. Which 1983 track by New Order was originally a B-side, but later became one of their most iconic songs?

3. What obscure 1986 track by Prince was a critical success but did not chart high commercially?

4. Which early 80s song by The Cure was overlooked but later became a fan favourite, "The Walk"?

5. What was the name of the track from *True Blue* by Madonna that was never released as a single but became a cult favourite?

6. Which 1980 song by Queen, featured on *The Game* album, was seen as a departure from their typical sound?

7. "The Chauffeur" by Duran Duran is known as a lesser-played track. From which album is it?

8. What 1982 track by The Human League was a B-side but has since been widely praised in electronic music circles?

9. Which overlooked track by U2 on *War* became a fan anthem in the years after its release?

10. What lesser-known song by George Michael, included on *Listen Without Prejudice*, was a standout for its jazz influences?

11. What experimental 1983 song by Kate Bush combined orchestral elements with rock and became a cult classic?

12. Which 1984 song by Talking Heads was a critical darling but failed to chart high?

13. What hidden gem from *Brothers in Arms* by Dire Straits gained significant critical praise but is not widely known?

14. Which 1985 track by The Smiths was released only as a limited 7-inch single and later became a deep cut?

15. What song by The Clash, often considered an album filler on *Combat Rock*, later became an anthem in punk rock circles?

16. What song by Madonna, which was released as a single in 1985, was considered too experimental for mainstream success?

17. Which 1986 Depeche Mode track, originally meant to be a filler, became a fan favourite despite poor initial reception?

18. What song from *Speak and Spell* by Depeche Mode is considered their most underappreciated early work?

19. Which song by the Pretenders was a slow burner and gained popularity only after its initial release?

20. What track from *Hysteria* by Def Leppard did not get the radio play other hits did, but remains one of their best?

21. Which 1982 track by Eurythmics, not a single, has since been recognized as a groundbreaking synth-pop anthem?

22. Which lesser-known track by A-ha from *Scoundrel Days* became a fan favourite and was considered one of their best compositions?

23. What overlooked 1983 song by The Police featured a reggae-inspired rhythm, but did not gain widespread attention?

24. What 1980 post-punk track by The Jam was initially met with mixed reviews but has since been hailed as one of their most innovative songs?

25. What 1988 song by The Stone Roses, long considered a non-single, has since become a defining track of the era?

Chapter 16 Answers:

1. *Station to Station*
2. "Blue Monday"
3. "Kiss"
4. "The Walk"
5. "Love Makes the World Go Round"
6. "Another One Bites the Dust"
7. *Rio*
8. "The Sound of the Crowd"
9. "Gloria"
10. "Cowboys and Angels"
11. "Sat in Your Lap"
12. "This Must Be the Place (Naive Melody)"
13. "Your Latest Trick"
14. "Shakespeare's Sister"
15. "Should I Stay or Should I Go"
16. "Love Don't Live Here Anymore"
17. "Strangelove"
18. "New Life"
19. "Back on the Chain Gang"
20. "Gods of War"

21. "This Is the House"
22. "Manhattan Skyline"
23. "De Do Do Do, De Da Da Da"
24. "That's Entertainment"
25. "I Am the Resurrection"

Chapter 17: The Underground Scene and Cult Favourites

Questions:

1. Which 1983 album by Bauhaus created an entire new wave of post-punk and goth music?

2. What 1985 album by R.E.M. was influential in shaping the indie rock genre in the US?

3. Which lesser-known band from the UK released the influential album *Parallel Lines*?

4. What underground track by Siouxsie and the Banshees became an anthem in the goth subculture?

5. What obscure 1987 song by The Smiths became a cult classic, despite not being widely known?

6. "A Forest" by The Cure was originally a deep-cut track in 1980. What song was it the B-side to?

7. Which 1984 album by The Cocteau Twins was one of the most influential in the shoegaze genre?

8. What track by The Jesus and Mary Chain from *Psychocandy* was considered too abrasive for

mainstream listeners but remains beloved in alternative rock circles?

9. Which 1982 track by The Fall is considered one of their most experimental works?

10. Which early 80s album by Sonic Youth was a landmark release in underground rock?

11. Which track by My Bloody Valentine from *Isn't Anything* became a staple of the shoegaze movement?

12. "Public Image" by Public Image Ltd was controversial for its departure from punk rock. What year did it release?

13. What 1981 album by Joy Division remains influential in gothic and post-punk scenes?

14. Which industrial band released *The Land of Rape and Honey* in 1988, shaping the sound of alternative metal?

15. What track by Nick Cave and the Bad Seeds was a defining moment in post-punk music in 1985?

16. Which 1986 album by Big Black became a hallmark in industrial rock?

17. What 1980 release by Gang of Four became a cornerstone for political punk rock?

18. What 1983 album by The Replacements is still revered in alternative rock circles for its raw emotion?

19. Which 1987 album by Dinosaur Jr. is often seen as one of the foundational works of indie rock?

20. Which 1989 album by Pixies heavily influenced the alt-rock movement in the 90s?

21. What band's 1985 album *The Queen Is Dead* is often cited as one of the greatest albums ever?

22. Which 1982 single by Bauhaus remains an iconic track in the goth scene?

23. Which 1983 song by The Sisters of Mercy became an anthem for alternative fans across the globe?

24. What 1980 album by Public Enemy, although controversial, would later influence rap and hip hop culture for years to come?

25. Which 1986 track by Dead Kennedys became iconic in the punk scene, although it was often censored by mainstream radio?

Chapter 17 Answers:

1. *In the Flat Field*
2. *Fables of the Reconstruction*
3. Blondie
4. "Spellbound"
5. "Please Please Please Let Me Get What I Want"
6. "The Drowning Man"
7. *Treasure*
8. "Just Like Honey"
9. "How I Wrote Elastic Man"
10. *Confusion Is Sex*
11. "Feed Me with Your Kiss"
12. 1978
13. *Closer*
14. Ministry
15. "The Mercy Seat"
16. *Songs About Fucking*
17. *Entertainment!*
18. *Let It Be*
19. *You're Living All Over Me*

20. *Surfer Rosa*
21. The Smiths
22. "Bela Lugosi's Dead"
23. "Temple of Love"
24. *Yo! Bum Rush the Show*
25. "Holiday in Cambodia"

Chapter 18: 80s Music Influences on Modern Artists

Questions:

1. Which 1982 album by Michael Jackson is often credited with influencing modern pop and R&B sounds?

2. "With or Without You" by U2 laid the groundwork for which modern band's atmospheric rock style?

3. Which 1981 single by Queen inspired future stadium rock bands like Coldplay and Muse?

4. What 1980 song by Blondie is regarded as a precursor to the integration of rap into pop music?

5. Prince's *1999* album directly influenced which modern artist's funk-inspired music?

6. Which New Wave band influenced artists like The Killers and Imagine Dragons with their 1983 hit "Blue Monday"?

7. What song by Talking Heads is considered foundational for indie rock bands like Arcade Fire?

8. Which 1980s track by Kate Bush inspired artists such as Florence Welch and Lorde?

9. The guitar riffs in The Smiths' songs are cited as a major influence for which Britpop band?

10. Depeche Mode's synth-driven sound in the 80s is considered pivotal for what modern electronic genre?

11. What track from Whitney Houston's debut album has been covered by numerous contemporary artists?

12. "Sweet Child o' Mine" by Guns N' Roses inspired the guitar style of which 2000s rock band?

13. Which Madonna song is frequently referenced by artists like Lady Gaga and Dua Lipa?

14. Tears for Fears' "Everybody Wants to Rule the World" is often sampled in modern electronic music. Which producer heavily draws from their sound?

15. The Cure's 80s goth-rock style influenced which American emo band?

16. What 1987 track by George Michael set a precedent for introspective pop albums in the 2000s?

17. Which industrial track by Nine Inch Nails from the late 80s paved the way for modern experimental rock?

18. "Take On Me" by A-ha inspired what modern animated music video trend?

19. Which Fleetwood Mac track gained renewed fame thanks to TikTok in the 2020s?

20. Eurythmics' 1983 song "Sweet Dreams (Are Made of This)" influenced what modern EDM artist?

21. "Don't You (Forget About Me)" by Simple Minds set the standard for what type of soundtrack song in films?

22. Which 1982 song by Marvin Gaye introduced a sound that influenced neo-soul?

23. The Pixies' use of quiet-loud dynamics in their 80s albums directly influenced which 90s grunge band?

24. What song by The Police became a template for sampling in 90s hip hop?

25. Which synth-pop duo influenced artists like Pet Shop Boys and Years & Years?

Chapter 18 Answers:

1. *Thriller*
2. Coldplay
3. "We Will Rock You"
4. "Rapture"
5. Bruno Mars
6. New Order
7. "Once in a Lifetime"
8. "Running Up That Hill"
9. Oasis
10. Synth-pop and EDM
11. "Greatest Love of All"
12. Foo Fighters
13. "Like a Prayer"
14. Kanye West
15. My Chemical Romance
16. "Father Figure"
17. "Head Like a Hole"
18. Anime-inspired music videos
19. "Dreams"
20. Avicii

21. Coming-of-age film soundtracks
22. "Sexual Healing"
23. Nirvana
24. "Every Breath You Take"
25. Erasure

Chapter 19: Unforgettable 80s Concerts and Tours

Questions:

1. What year did Live Aid take place, and which two cities hosted the event?

2. Which legendary performer famously moonwalked during a televised concert in 1983?

3. What massive 1981 Rolling Stones tour set a new standard for stadium rock performances?

4. Which 1985 concert by Bruce Springsteen is often cited as one of the best live performances of all time?

5. What tour by U2 supported their *The Joshua Tree* album and became a global sensation?

6. Which Queen concert at Wembley Stadium in 1986 is remembered as one of their most iconic performances?

7. Madonna's *Blond Ambition Tour* in 1990 was groundbreaking, but which 80s tour solidified her as a live performer?

8. What controversial song did Prince perform during his *Purple Rain* tour, shocking audiences?

9. Which 1989 tour by The Cure featured elaborate gothic stage designs that influenced live performances for years?

10. What 1987 Michael Jackson tour became one of the highest-grossing tours of the decade?

11. Which artist performed to over 3.5 million people at their 1988 "Monsters of Rock" tour in Moscow?

12. What 1983 David Bowie tour was dubbed "The Serious Moonlight Tour"?

13. Which band closed their 1986 tour with an emotional farewell concert in Birmingham, later reuniting in the 90s?

14. What 1985 performance by Tina Turner was considered her comeback moment?

15. Which New Wave band's 1984 tour was documented in the concert film *Stop Making Sense*?

16. What famous "Unplugged" performance by an 80s band later inspired MTV's popular series?

17. Which rock band performed at the first Monsters of Rock festival in Donnington in 1980?

18. Who headlined the first Glastonbury Festival in the 80s?

19. What 1983 tour by Cyndi Lauper was her breakout as a headliner?

20. Which band's reunion concert in 1985 at Live Aid shocked the audience with their chemistry?

21. What famous benefit concert series was organized by George Harrison in 1982?

22. Which Fleetwood Mac tour in the late 80s supported their *Tango in the Night* album?

23. What was the name of the 1989 Janet Jackson tour that established her as a live force?

24. Which stadium tour in 1987 was backed by iconic inflatable pigs?

25. What 1986 concert at Wembley Stadium is regarded as the pinnacle of Madonna's early career?

Chapter 19 Answers:

1. 1985, London and Philadelphia
2. Michael Jackson
3. *Tattoo You* tour
4. *Born in the U.S.A. Tour*
5. *The Joshua Tree Tour*
6. *Magic Tour*
7. *Like a Virgin Tour*
8. "Darling Nikki"
9. *Kiss Me, Kiss Me, Kiss Me* tour
10. *Bad World Tour*
11. Metallica
12. David Bowie
13. ELO (Electric Light Orchestra)
14. *Private Dancer Tour*
15. Talking Heads
16. Eric Clapton's Unplugged (inspired by U2)
17. AC/DC
18. Van Morrison
19. *She's So Unusual Tour*

20. Led Zeppelin
21. *The Concert for Bangladesh*
22. Fleetwood Mac
23. *Rhythm Nation 1814 Tour*
24. Pink Floyd
25. Madonna

Chapter 20: The Most Obscure 80s Bands You've Never Heard Of

Questions:

1. Which British band released *Jeopardy* in 1980 and is credited with influencing post-punk?

2. What obscure band from Manchester released the album *Script of the Bridge* in 1983?

3. Which Canadian new wave band had a minor hit with "Echo Beach"?

4. What 1980s Scottish band gained a cult following for their atmospheric soundscapes?

5. Which American band released the influential *Double Nickels on the Dime* in 1984?

6. What obscure Australian band is known for their single "The Unguarded Moment"?

7. Which 1983 single by Kajagoogoo became a one-hit wonder?

8. What German electronic band was a precursor to synthwave, releasing *Computer World* in 1981?

9. Which Sheffield band released the influential but underappreciated album *Soul Mining*?

10. What American indie band released *Zen Arcade* in 1984, influencing 90s grunge?
11. Which post-punk band is best known for their 1981 single "Party Fears Two"?
12. What 1980s act released *Ocean Rain*, considered one of the best albums of the decade?
13. Which experimental band from Wales gained a cult following with *Colossal Youth*?
14. What was the name of the group formed by Joy Division members after Ian Curtis's death?
15. Which 80s industrial band gained fame for their track "Bela Lugosi's Dead"?
16. What Dutch band had a minor hit with "Twilight Zone" in 1982?
17. Which cult Irish band released *A Pagan Place* in 1984?
18. What 1987 track by The Jesus and Mary Chain gained traction in the indie scene?
19. Which Liverpool-based band released *Crocodiles* in 1980?
20. What 1985 album by Prefab Sprout is now considered a hidden gem?
21. What obscure 80s band sang the quirky song "Major Tom (Coming Home)"?

22. Which 80s art-rock band is best known for their album *Remain in Light*?

23. What lesser-known 1983 band gained a following with their gothic single "Temple of Love"?

24. What 1982 band was influential in blending ska and punk rock?

25. What 1989 indie rock band released *Doolittle*, gaining massive critical acclaim?

Chapter 20 Answers:

1. The Sound
2. The Chameleons
3. Martha and the Muffins
4. Cocteau Twins
5. Minutemen
6. The Church
7. "Too Shy"
8. Kraftwerk
9. The The
10. Hüsker Dü
11. The Associates
12. Echo & the Bunnymen
13. Young Marble Giants
14. New Order
15. Bauhaus
16. Golden Earring
17. The Waterboys
18. "Just Like Honey"
19. Echo & the Bunnymen
20. *Steve McQueen*

21. Peter Schilling
22. Talking Heads
23. The Sisters of Mercy
24. The Specials
25. Pixies

Printed in Great Britain
by Amazon